Crime Scenes

John Townsend

Chicago, Illinois

For information, address the publisher:
Raintree, 100 N. LaSalle, Suite 1200, Chicago, IL 60602
Customer Service: 888-363-4266
Visit our website at www.raintreelibrary.com

Printed and bound in China by South China Printing Company.
08 07 06 05 04
10 9 8 7 6 5 4 3 2 1

Library of Congress Cataloging-in-Publication Data
Townsend, John, 1955-
    Crime scenes / John Townsend.
        p. cm. -- (True crime)
    Includes bibliographical references and index.
    ISBN 1-4109-1092-X (library binding) -- ISBN 1-4109-1171-3(pbk.)
    1. Crime scene searches--Juvenile literature. 2. Evidence,
Criminal--Juvenile literature.
    3. Criminal investigation--Juvenile literature. 4. Forensic
sciences--Vocational guidance
    --Juvenile literature.   I. Title. II. Series: Townsend, John, 1955-
. True crime.
    HV8073.8.T68 2004
    363.25'2--dc22

2004012877

Acknowledgments
Alamy pp. **17** (Plain picture/Kummerow T.), **13** (Shout); Associated Press pp. **20–21, 28** (Boulder Police department); Corbis Sygma pp. **9** (Lewis Alan), **40–41** (Klein Stephane), **11** (Outlook); Corbis pp. **30** (Bojan Brecelj), **31** (Gyori Antoine), **38–39, 42** (Harcourt Education Ltd), **5** (William Whitehurst); Forensic Alliance p. **22** (JRA Smith); Getty Images News & Sport pp. **28–29**; Getty Images p. **24** (Taxi); John Callan/Shout pp. **4, 6, 8, 12, 14, 15, 16, 16–17, 19, 21, 23, 26–27, 32, 33, 40, 42–43**; Kobal Collection p. **7** (CBS-TV/Touchstone/Voets, Robert); PA Photos p. **25** (EPA); Photodisc/ Harcourt Education Ltd pp. **25, 37, 41**; Science Photo Library pp. **27, 39, 36–37** (VVG), **33** (Bluestone), **26** (Dr Jeremy Burgess), **35** (John McLean), **34** (Laguna Design), **10** (Pascal Goetgheluck), **31** (Roger Harris), **18, 43** (Tek Image), **6, 36** (Volker Steger/Peter Arnold Inc).
Cover photograph of footprint reproduced with permission of Forensic Alliance

Every effort has been made to contact copyright holders of any material reproduced in this book. Any omissions will be rectified in subsequent printings if notice is given to the publishers.

The paper used to print this book comes from sustainable resources.

Contents

Any words appearing in the text in **bold** are explained in the glossary. You can also look out for them in the "Word Bank" at the bottom of each page.

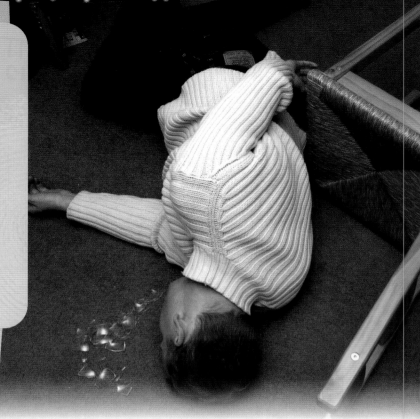

A crime scene is . . .

Any place where a crime has been committed—for example, a room, a field, or a car. It will contain **evidence** that a crime has taken place. This book looks at murder scenes in particular.

A dead body is lying in the middle of a room. The door is locked from the inside. A chair is on its side. There is no blood, no smoking gun, and no sign of a struggle. The body has no wounds, but there is broken glass nearby. What happened?

If you had to **investigate,** you would need to answer many questions. Is this the scene of a crime? Is it a murder? Every clue matters if you are going to find out the truth. Maybe the man stood on the chair to change a lightbulb. Perhaps he had wet hands and was killed by an electric shock.

Word Bank

evidence   facts pointing to what happened
fibers   tiny threads

A closer look

Things are not always what they seem. There are tiny blue **fibers** on the window frame—from someone's jeans. What about the faint shoe print on the windowsill? A closer look at the body shows something else. There is a tiny needle mark behind the knee, where poison was injected. This was not an accident, but rather a planned murder.

Some crime scenes are not what they seem to be. It is only after a very careful search that a crime scene may begin to show its hidden secrets. The experts' secret is knowing just what to look for.

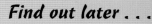

Find out later . . .

What do we all leave behind wherever we go?

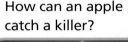

How can an apple catch a killer?

When do detectives need a dog's nose at a crime scene?

At the Scene of the Crime

On television, police work looks easy. The detectives arrive at the scene of a murder, begin dusting for prints, and then spot a **vital** clue. It soon leads them to the killer.

Arriving at a real scene

True crime is not quite like that. First, the scene must be sealed off. Nothing can be touched. It then takes hours and hours of careful work to find out what may have happened. Many items from the crime scene are sealed in bags. They are sent to scientists in the **laboratory** known as a "**crime lab**." It is then up to these scientists to find the answers.

Did you know?

The study of tiny details at a crime scene is called **forensic** science. A scientist named Edmund Locard figured out that when two objects make contact, they **transfer** traces of evidence. Tiny particles such as specks of dust get moved from one thing to another. Most of this "trace evidence" can only be seen under a **microscope**.

A forensic expert looks for clues on a shoe.

Word Bank

forensic detailed scientific investigation to help solve crimes

The search

Sometimes it is difficult to figure out the size of a crime scene. It might be a single room or a whole house. In the case of a murder, the killer may have left **traces** of his or her presence in many rooms. If someone was killed in one place and then taken somewhere else, there could be many crime scenes. If the body was carried in a car, that also becomes part of the crime scene.

Often, the most important **evidence** is close to the place where the murder took place. The skill is in finding the exact spot.

Edmund Locard

Edmund Locard was a policeman in Lyon, France, about a hundred years ago. In 1910 he became a **professor** of forensic science. He set up the first police crime laboratory. In 1912 he discovered that fingerprints were important pieces of evidence. In 1920 he explained how all people leave tiny traces behind them wherever they go.

The TV show *Crime Scene Investigation (CSI): Miami* is about a team of forensic scientists and investigators.

microscope   instrument for magnifying tiny objects
trace   very small mark, sign, or substance that is left behind

Evidence in the ashes

Some criminals set fire to crime scenes to destroy all the evidence. Investigators can still find a lot of evidence, even after a fire. They can soon tell where and how a fire started. Then they search through the ashes for more clues.

Questions and answers

A dead body is found. It seems **suspicious,** so the police are called. As soon as they arrive, they must ask key questions:
- What has happened and where?
- How big is the area to be sealed off?
- Who is involved?
- When did the murder happen?

The scene has to be cleared of all people. Any onlookers have to be kept far away. It may not be obvious who the **victim** is or if there are any witnesses. Two important types of **evidence** at a crime scene are information given by witnesses and items found near the body. The time of the murder may have to be figured out by experts at the **crime lab.**

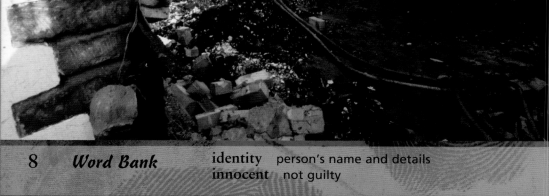

Word Bank   identity   person's name and details
innocent   not guilty

Recording clues

Crime scene investigators must find clues to five big questions.

- Who has been murdered?
- How did the murder take place?
- Did it happen here, or was another crime scene involved?
- Why did the murder happen?
- Who did it?

The evidence collected can:
- link a **suspect** with a scene or a victim;
- prove the **identity** of a victim or suspect;
- support what a witness says;
- support someone who is a suspect but is **innocent**.

Cause of death

The cause of death is not always what it seems at first. Someone may have tried to set up the scene to **mislead** the police.

The police try to find out if the death falls into one of five groups:
- natural;
- accidental;
- suicide;
- murder;
- uncertain.

The handling, packaging, and labeling of evidence at a crime scene has to be done correctly. Otherwise, it cannot be used as evidence in court.

Calling the experts

Photographers and medical experts also come to a crime scene to collect **evidence.**

The photographer at a crime scene has to act quickly. Before anything is touched or moved, photos of the whole scene are taken from all angles. In a room, the photographer will take pictures from each corner.

Photographer's checklist

☑ Photograph entire area before anyone enters.
☑ Photograph **victims**, people, and nearby vehicles.
☑ Photograph entire scene with wide and close-up shots.
☑ Photograph all major items of evidence before they are moved.
☑ Make detailed notes for each photograph.

Information technology help

Modern **digital photos** are very helpful for crime scene investigators. Computer images can be enlarged easily. The latest software is used to help identify or match pieces of evidence. This process is much faster than methods used a few years ago.

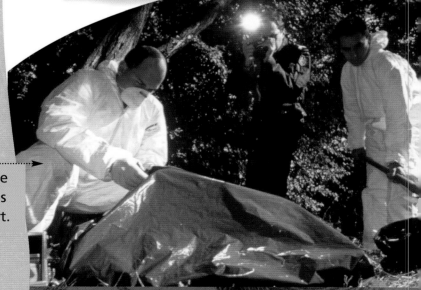

Photos of a crime scene are used as evidence in court.

autopsy   examination of a dead body to find the cause of death

Medical experts

The photographer must work closely with the rest of the team. The team must measure the crime scene and draw plans. Each shoe print must be photographed with a ruler beside it to show its size.

In the case of a **suspicious** death, a medical expert will be needed. The body must not be touched until a full medical examination has taken place. Even hanging bodies cannot be cut down.

Once all the details about the body have been carefully noted, it is taken away for a more detailed examination. This is called an **autopsy.** The body may be cut open and the organs taken out to be studied for clues that explain the cause of death.

The body

A body has to be taken from the crime scene very carefully. It must be wrapped in a **sterile** sheet to preserve any evidence on it. It is then put into a body bag and taken to the **mortuary** for the full autopsy.

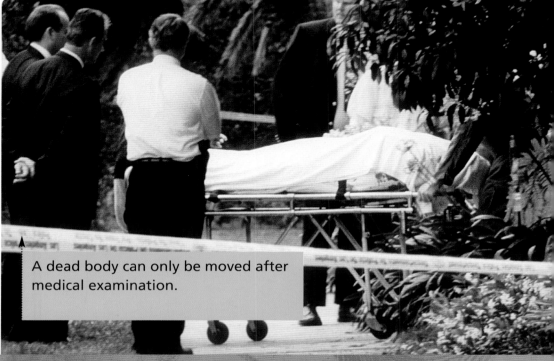

A dead body can only be moved after medical examination.

mortuary   place where dead bodies are kept until burial
sterile   completely clean

Whenever you touch something, you leave a faint smear of grease, dust, or sweat behind. The **unique** pattern on your fingers stays on everything you touch. It is an autograph that says, "I was here."

A thumb points to the killer

In 1905 a shop in Deptford, England, was broken into. The owner was killed and his wife lay almost dead upstairs. The **victims** had been woken in the night and attacked. Police found a thumbprint on an empty cashbox.

A **suspect** was arrested, and his thumbprint matched the one on the cashbox. This made **legal** history because it was the first time fingerprints had **convinced** a **jury**. The suspect was **convicted** of murder and hanged.

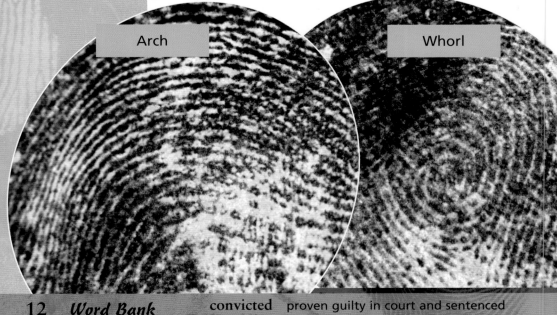

Arch

Whorl

Word Bank   convicted   proven guilty in court and sentenced
               convince   to persuade

Progress

It used to take the police hours to match fingerprints to a set in their records. Today, computers can compare one set of fingerprints against half a million others in less than a second. The patterns for fingerprints are put into four groups.

An expert looks for fingerprints.

1. Arches: Formed by ridges running across the finger. About 5 percent of people have this print.

2. Whorls: About 30 percent of fingerprints form a complete oval, often in a spiral pattern.

3. Loops: These have a stronger curve than arches. About 60 percent of fingerprints have loops.

4. A mixture of all the patterns.

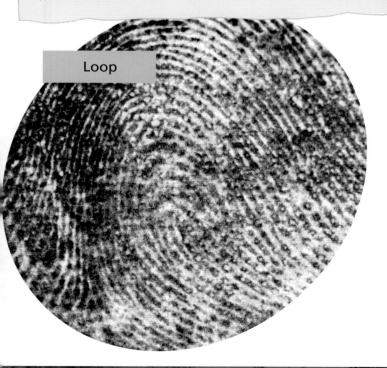

Loop

First time in the United States

In 1910 Thomas Jennings became the first person in the United States to be convicted using fingerprint **evidence.** When he broke into a home in Chicago and shot the owner, he left four clear prints in wet paint. Fingerprint experts told the jury this was proof that Jennings was the killer. After this case, the use of fingerprinting spread across the United States.

legal   to do with the law
unique   only one of it in the whole world

Making the right impression

In 1984 Juanita Gillette died suddenly in California. Her husband said she had mixed up her medication. The police began asking questions and took a closer look. An **autopsy** on Juanita found that she had not died from drug poisoning. Something else must have killed her, but the police were not sure what.

Police searched the scene of Juanita's death again and found a plastic laundry bag. When they looked closely, it seemed to have a nose print in it. The **impression** of the dead woman's face was still on the bag. She had been **suffocated**. This **evidence** led to the **conviction** of her husband for murder.

A dusting brush and gloves are **vital** tools for a crime scene investigator.

Word Bank

conviction   when a court finds someone guilty of a crime
impression   mark or print left behind

Washington state, 1994

An **intruder** beat James McCann to death in his home. At the crime scene, the police found a print that looked like an ear. When they arrested a **suspect,** they took his ear print by pressing it against glass.

Scientists said the suspect was a "likely source" of the ear print at the crime scene. But this evidence was not allowed to be used in court because it was not thought to be as **reliable** as fingerprints. **Forensic** experts think ear prints could one day be used as evidence in court, if suspects happen to leave any behind. So be careful if you listen at a door!

Not smart enough

In 1968 a thief in Israel tried to be smart. He took off his socks to put over his hands so he would not leave fingerprints behind. But he did not know that toe prints are **unique,** too. The police arrested him by tracing the prints left by his bare feet!

All ear patterns are different—just like fingerprints.

reliable   something that can be trusted
suffocate   to choke or kill by stopping breathing

Telltale prints

Human skin is covered in tiny lines, marks, and patterns. Each person's hand is **unique.** Even identical twins have different palm prints. Kneeling down with bare knees will leave knee prints that could also be traced. Bare feet can get a criminal into trouble, too. That is because the soles of our feet have shapes and patterns that are unique to each person.

Tongues, lips, cheeks, and many other parts of the body can leave a print behind that crime scene investigators might find and match to a **suspect.** New technology helps to find, preserve, and match **impressions** made by the human body.

No two shoe prints are exactly alike.

cast   to shape like something else using a mold

Footprints

If a footprint at a crime scene is left in soft surfaces such as mud, sand, and snow, a **cast** can be made. A computer can then closely look at every little detail of the print. The soles of shoes and sneakers get worn or marked by sharp objects. Cuts, scratches, or tiny stones wedged in the tread leave unique marks.

The impression left by a shoe can be just as detailed as a fingerprint. All the police have to do is examine their suspects' shoes until they find a match. The suspect will have to prove that someone else was wearing the shoes!

Snow prints

Sometimes investigators use liquid **sulfur** to make a mold of an impression left in the snow. The liquid sulfur quickly cools as it touches the snow. It immediately freezes in the shape of the print.

Making a cast of a footprint in snow has to be done carefully since it can be easily damaged.

sulfur   yellow substance sometimes used to make gunpowder

Blood

The sight of blood upsets many people. For crime scene investigators, it is full of useful information.

Blood types

In 1901 scientists found out that there are four main human blood groups. These are called A, B, AB, and O. Types A and O are the most common groups. Type AB is the most rare.

Bloodstains

For over a hundred years, scientists have been able to tell whether blood came from a human or an animal. They could also tell the human blood group to which a stain belonged. By 1950 they could tell if it came from a male or a female.

Today's technology means a speck of blood can be matched to a particular person. That is why many murderers try to get rid of any blood, especially their own. But however hard a killer tries to clean up, tiny specks of blood will be left behind, and investigators will find them.

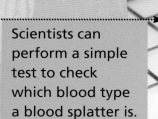

Scientists can perform a simple test to check which blood type a blood splatter is.

Word Bank   analysis   careful study and examination

Reading the signs

Investigators study blood patterns to tell how blood left the body. This is called blood-pattern **analysis**.

Blood can drip, spray, or ooze from a large wound or it can fly off a weapon. At a crime scene, blood may be found as:

- drops on a surface;
- splashes from blood flying through the air and hitting a surface at an angle;
- pools or smears around the body, which can show if it has been dragged;
- spurts from a major **artery** or **vein** in the body.

The police use this information to figure out how each wound happened and what sort of weapon was used.

When blood falls from a body, it can land in many different ways.

vein   tube in the body that carries blood to the heart

The case of O. J. Simpson

On the night of July 12, 1994, Nicole Simpson and Ronald Goldman were found dead. They were covered in blood and were outside Nicole's home in California. She was once married to the famous football player O. J. Simpson.

Police rushed to O. J. Simpson's house on the night of the murder. They saw a bloodstain on the door of his white Ford Bronco. A trail of blood led up to his house, and Simpson had a cut on his left hand. Blood splashes at the crime scene suggested that the killer had been cut on the left hand and had left a trail of blood. O. J. Simpson was arrested for the murders.

Trial of the century

The Simpson trial became one of the most famous criminal trials in history. It lasted nine months, with eleven lawyers defending the **suspect**. It cost over $20 million to defend O. J. Simpson. The way crime scene investigators had handled the blood samples decided the outcome of the whole trial.

O. J. Simpson (right) talks to his lawyer in court.

Word Bank   defense team   lawyers in court who try to show that a suspect is not guilty

Evidence and trial

Forensic tests showed that some drops of blood at the crime scene were Simpson's. His blood was also found near footprints made by a rare type of shoe. Simpson wore this type and size of shoe. There were **traces** of both **victims'** blood inside Simpson's car and house.

A bloodstained glove at the crime scene matched another stained with Simpson's blood, found at his house. It seemed that the **evidence** against Simpson would **convict** him. But his **defense team** attacked the crime scene investigators for bad work. Blood samples had been badly handled so were not **reliable,** they argued. The **jury** found Simpson not guilty.

Improvements

All crime scene investigators now have to:

- wear **latex** gloves, surgical masks, and full **sterile** suits (below);
- label all blood samples;
- package dry samples and stained clothes in bags;
- clean their hands with bleach and **dispose** of suits.

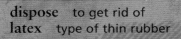

dispose   to get rid of
latex   type of thin rubber

Blood but no body

Caren Campano disappeared from her home in Oklahoma City in 1992. Her husband, Chris Campano, let crime scene investigators look around the house. They found a brown patch on the bedroom carpet. Tests showed that it was human blood.

A closer look around the house found tiny splatter patterns of blood. These showed that someone had been hit many times with a blunt object.

Even if a crime scene appears to be spotless, a special chemical called luminol can make tiny specks of blood show up. When luminol is sprayed around a room, even old bloodstains will start to glow blue or green when ultraviolet light is shone on them.

Luminol can reveal hidden secrets at a crime scene.

dental   to do with teeth

Answers in blood

From the blood they found in the Campano house, police figured out two things. First, a person the size of Caren Campano would have lost at least 40 percent of her blood. She could not have lived through that loss. Second, by taking blood samples from her family, police showed the blood was almost certainly Caren's.

The police searched all around the garden and nearby wasteland until they found a skeleton. The teeth matched Caren's **dental** records. Her skull had been smashed. This matched up with the **evidence** from the crime scene. Chris Campano was arrested and later **convicted** of the murder of his wife.

Bloodstains can help car crash investigators figure out what caused an accident.

Crash scenes

Blood is not only important at murder scenes. Sometimes a car crash can be a real mystery. Crash investigators have to examine the scene carefully to find out what happened. This may involve looking closely at bloodstains left by injured people. In a **hit-and-run** case, a **suspect's** car could be tested for signs of the **victim's** blood.

The study of diseases and how they affect the body is called **pathology.** Someone who does an **autopsy** on a body to find the cause of death is called a **pathologist.** A **forensic** pathologist has to examine the body of a murder **victim** for clues.

Dealing with death

A body is X-rayed, weighed, and measured. Notes are taken of all marks on it, such as old and new injuries, scars, and tattoos. Hair and **fibers** are collected from the body and under the fingernails. Fingerprints are also taken. Then the body might be opened up to see what clues are inside.

Did you know?

Right after death, the body goes limp and floppy. But after between fifteen minutes and fifteen hours, the muscles stiffen. This is called rigor mortis. The body stays **rigid** for a while before the rigor mortis wears off. It may take as long as ten hours for the body to go limp again.

Pathologists must make sure a body is photographed and labeled.

pathologist   person who studies disease and injury and their effects on the body

Pathologist's checklist

- ☑ **rigor mortis**
- ☑ bruising
- ☑ body temperature
- ☑ rotting
- ☑ drying of the **tissues**

Finding answers

The temperature of the liver and brain can suggest how long ago a person died. After death, body temperature falls by 34.7 °F (1.5 °C) per hour until it is the same as the surroundings. The body temperature will depend on the amount of body fat, any bleeding, the victim's clothes, and if the body was found indoors or outdoors. The weather conditions will affect how quickly the body cools.

Inside information

A pathologist will often look inside a victim's stomach. This gives clues about what happened just before he or she died. A light meal may stay in the body for about two hours, but a heavy meal could last up to six hours. How far food has passed through the **intestine** can show how long after eating food the victim died.

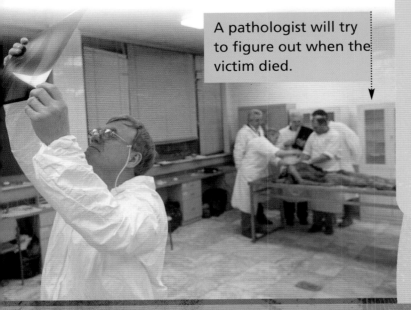

A pathologist will try to figure out when the victim died.

rigor mortis   stiffening of the muscles that happens soon after death

Dead but alive

If flies get to a dead body, they lay eggs on it. These soon hatch into maggots. The size of the maggots can be a clue to the time of death. Finding many sorts of insects in the body can mean that it was moved from one **habitat** to another. Some insects only lay eggs during daylight, so they can be a help in finding the time of death.

Time of death

Figuring out when a **victim** died is not easy. Nature provides a few answers. Insects can be a big help to a **pathologist.** New Zealand police found a body in a car in Auckland in early 1993. Fly maggots had hatched in the body. Their size showed that death must have taken place at least eight or nine days before.

Investigators took the temperature inside the car and then hatched out maggots in some meat at the same temperature. They were able to pinpoint the time of death as the early hours of Christmas Day 1992. This **evidence** agreed with other key details when the case went to court.

bacteria   tiny bugs that can only be seen under a microscope

Immediately after death, **bacteria** that live in the body get to work. They start to **dissolve** the organs. This makes gas, which causes the body to swell up until the gas escapes. The face darkens and liquids escape through the nose and mouth. These clues can all help a pathologist to tell how long a person has been dead.

Insect evidence

Mike Rubenstein called the police in December 1993. He reported the deaths of his relatives in a cabin in Summit, Canada. Crime scene investigators found the rotting bodies of three people. They were a man, a woman, and a four-year-old child. Rubenstein said the cabin had been empty a month ago, when he was last there.

Bacteria that live inside the gut can be seen with a **microscope**.

A pathologist figured out how much the bodies had begun to rot. The size of insects inside them showed the time of death was a month before. That was exactly when Rubenstein said he last visited the cabin. The police arrested him, and he was soon **convicted** of the murders.

dissolve   to break down into a liquid
habitat   natural home of an animal

The exact time and place a person died cannot always be discovered. If the crime scene or the body have been disturbed, important clues will be lost. At 5:52 A.M. on the day after Christmas 1996, the mother of six-year-old JonBenét Ramsey called the police. She could not find JonBenét in her Colorado house. She did find a **ransom** note saying her daughter had been kidnapped.

The police visited the house, but at the time no one knew it was a murder scene. Objects were moved before they could be photographed. The ransom note was moved and handled. Friends of the family were allowed into the house to roam around freely.

Ruining the crime scene

Police have learned the hard way how to protect a crime scene. In court, if any evidence is shown to be false or damaged, the **prosecution's** case can fall apart. That is why the scene of a crime is now sealed off immediately. This stops people from destroying vital evidence before the **forensic** team arrives.

Police still do not know who murdered JonBenét.

Word Bank   prosecution   team of lawyers who try to prove someone is guilty of a crime

Discovery

JonBenét was found murdered in the basement. Her parents picked her up and covered her with a blanket. This **interfered** with **trace evidence** as well as her body temperature. The body had **rigor mortis** at the time, although there was no expert there to give an official assessment.

Because it was Christmas, the **pathologist** did not arrive for six hours. By then, many people had trampled over the crime scene. It had been at least fourteen hours since JonBenét had died, and maybe as long as twenty-two hours. The exact time of death could never be proven, and **vital** evidence had been destroyed.

Mistakes

The murder of JonBenét Ramsey has never been solved. The case was big news. The police were not used to this sort of crime in such a quiet neighborhood. They were blamed for not being careful enough with the crime scene. Important evidence was missed, ruined, or even lost.

The crime scene: the Ramsey house in Colorado.

ransom   payment demanded for the release of a prisoner

Clues in the bones

An adult human body has 206 bones. Together they weigh about 12 lb (5.5 kg) for an average male and almost 10 lb (4.5 kg) for an average female. Human bones have often told police a lot about the victim and even about the murderer. Police may even be able to tell if a killer was right- or left-handed!

A crime scene can sometimes be many years old. Perhaps the only thing left after a murder long ago is a shallow grave. The **victim's** bones have to tell the whole story. By laying out the skeleton, a **pathologist** can tell two main things.

"I can tell if the person was a male or female. The male **pelvis** is narrower than the female pelvis, and parts of the skull are larger in males. Also, I can tell the rough age of the person. In young people, bones are still growing or joining up. In older people, diseases such as arthritis or worn-down joints and teeth can give clues to how old the person was." PATHOLOGIST

Skeleton secrets

A close look at a skeleton tells the police many things about a murder victim. They look for the following information about the victim:

- Past accidents: If a bone has been broken in the past, hospital records might help to identify the victim.
- Ethnic group: Sometimes the skull around the nose and eye sockets can give clues to the shape of the face and possibly the person's ethnic group.
- Height: One quick clue is that our height is about five times the length of our **humerus.** Other bones in the leg can help show how tall someone was.
- Body type: Bones can help police tell if a person was slim, medium-sized, or heavy.

Word Bank   fracture   break or crack
humerus   bone in the upper arm

Telltale signs

Bones can sometimes show how a person died. The skull or other bones may show signs of a knife cut, bullet hole, a blunt weapon **fracture,** or even saw marks if the body was cut up. Sometimes bones will show **evidence** of poisoning if they are tested for **toxic** chemicals.

Pathologists can find out a lot about a murder victim from his or her skeleton.

This skull shows the victim was shot in the head.

pelvis   part of the skeleton, including the hips and lower back

Teeth

Your teeth say a lot about you. If a dentist has done work on them, they say even more. That is because dentists keep careful records of the work they do. The shapes, sizes, gaps, angles, and patterns of people's teeth are as **unique** as their fingerprints. If a body's teeth are matched against **dental** records, the police can identify the **victim.**

A killer's teeth can also leave clues. Bite marks can be traced. The teeth marks in an apple can be matched to a **suspect's** teeth. **Saliva** on gum can also be matched to a suspect.

Hungry criminals

Sometimes a criminal leaves a bite mark at a crime scene. Bite marks can be traced to the mouth that made them. Many thieves have carelessly left something like an apple core behind at a robbery. This evidence is all the crime scene investigator needs.

Many criminals have been caught because they bit something or someone at the crime scene.

saliva   fluid made in the mouth

Calling the dentist

Forensic dentists study bite marks at the scene of a crime. They can soon tell if it is a human or animal bite. If dentists make a mold from a bite mark, they can study every detail. Using computer images, they can see the exact way a suspect bites. Chipped or broken teeth in the mold can be checked against a suspect's teeth or dental records.

One murderer who left his bite at the crime scene tried to remove all **evidence.** How? Carmine Calabro took out all his teeth so he would not get caught. It did not work!

The exact shape of each tooth and the gaps in between are different in every person.

Teeth that tell

In a fight, a killer may bite his or her victim (above). Bite marks can tell the police:

- the shape of the killer's mouth;
- if there are any loose or broken teeth;
- the width and thickness of the teeth;
- if there are gaps or missing teeth;
- the curves of biting edges;
- if he or she has had any unusual dental work.

This evidence could be enough to **convict** someone.

Getting a picture

Modern computer **graphics** save the police a lot of time and effort. They can turn **digital photos** of a human skull into a picture of a face. The image can be put on posters to ask for the public's help. Some of these images have shown an amazing likeness to victims.

Bones that talk

Every murderer faces a question: What does he or she do with the body? A dead body will soon be found. Once the police have the body, it may give away many clues. Killers try to cover their tracks and keep the police guessing. They have tried many ways to get rid of dead bodies.

Many will bury them, but human bones can be uncovered again many years later. Even the old grave of a murder **victim** is a crime scene. The police must **investigate** and try to find out who the victim and the killer were.

Computers can now turn digital photos of a human skull into a picture of a face.

digital photos   photos made using computer software rather than photographic film

Making a face

A human skull can give clues about who the victim may have been. Experts can now make an image of what the face looked like. Using these images, they can then make a 3D model of the dead person.

By asking the public to identify a model face, the police have solved a number of mysteries. People have come forward to say, "I knew that person."

The first step is to figure out the shape of the face, using clay to build up the **features.** Hair found with a skull can give a good color match. Then they just need to fit a wig.

Looking older

Police face a problem when they look for people who have been missing for a long time. The person would now look different. What would they look like today? Computers can show us how a face ages and give a new "older" picture of the person.

A **forensic** scientist makes a model face by studying a victim's skull.

features   main parts of the face such as the nose, eyes, and chin

35

Leeds robbers: forensic evidence

- Some cash boxes leak purple security dye if they are broken open. This was found on the Leeds suspects' clothes and on the cash they were carrying.
- Tiny pieces of smashed glass from the crime scenes were found on tools and in the suspects' shoes.
- Rare tiny nylon fibers from the suspects' gloves were at the crime scenes.

A crime scene is like a huge puzzle. The pieces may be scattered everywhere.

Hunting for clues

Some clues are so small they cannot be seen. Tiny **fibers**, hair, or skin **cells** can be the last pieces to make the whole picture fit together. A gang from Leeds, in England, carried out 32 armed robberies in 2000. They stole over $1.7 million in cash.

The police had to match up hundreds of pieces of **evidence** to prove that some **suspects** were at the crime scenes. At last the puzzle fit together. Eight men were **convicted** in 2003 and sent to prison for a total of 93 years among them.

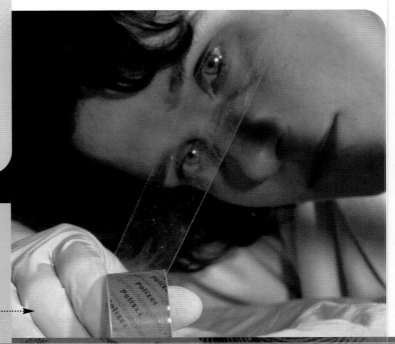

A crime scene investigator looks for tiny fibers or hair that may help convict a killer.

jury   group of people who decide if someone is guilty
pollen   fine grains, like dust, made by a flower or tree

The final piece

The first case to use a special test to match human hairs was in 1958 in Canada.

Sixteen-year-old Gaetane Bouchard was found murdered. A witness saw her by a fence with her boyfriend, John Vollman, just before she died. Flakes of paint from the fence were found in Vollman's car. So were **traces** of the **victim's** lipstick on some chocolate in the glove compartment.

But it was a hair in the victim's hand that **convinced** the **jury.** It was proven to belong to Vollman. It was evidence that Gaetane had fought with him as he killed her.

Tiny proof

The police can sometimes tell if a body has been moved from the murder scene. Tiny seeds and **pollen** from a very rare tree were found on a body in 1960. But how could they be matched to the suspect? Simple. The suspect had that very tree in his garden. It was enough proof to convict him of murder.

Pollen under a **microscope.**

A single hair at a crime scene can be enough to convict someone.

Bullets

When people are shot, the bullet inside them contains a lot of information. **Ballistics** experts can examine the bullet and figure out the exact gun that fired it. Tiny scratches on the bullet can match marks inside the barrel of the gun.

Looking at the crime scene can also tell experts exactly where the gun was fired. They can detect gunpowder on bodies, in walls, and on the gun itself. The experts also look for **cartridge** cases. These can give more details about the gun, possibly helping to match it to other crimes.

When bullets fly

If a crime scene is full of fired bullets, the **forensic** team studies every single one (below). They can tell how many guns were fired, how many times, and from where. This information can then be matched to statements from witnesses. A picture of the crime can start to build up.

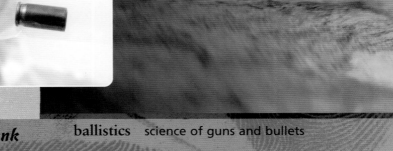

ballistics   science of guns and bullets

Bulletproof

Numbers stamped on bullets can show where they were bought and, sometimes, who bought them. Computer records store much of this information. Some criminals try to file these numbers off their bullets.

Even if the police can prove that a **suspect's** gun fired the killing bullet, they still have to prove who pulled the trigger. A suspect could say that another person fired the gun.

That is where the **crime lab** can come up with answers. Anyone who fires a gun will get tiny amounts of gunpowder or scorch marks on his or her hands and clothes. The scientists just have to find it and match it to **traces** at the crime scene.

Not foolproof

One problem for the forensic team is that anyone in a room where a gun is fired will get powder, or "gun **residue**," on them. It does not mean they are guilty. More **evidence** is needed to build up the full picture.

A close look at a gun can show when it was last fired.

Sniffing out evidence

The police use a lot of high-tech equipment at crime scenes to find hidden clues. But one piece is still fairly simple: a dog's nose. Some dogs, such as bloodhounds, have a really good sense of smell. They can be trained to find clues.

"Sniffer dogs" have been used for many years to find drugs or to track down criminals on the run. They are also good at sniffing out explosives or firemaking equipment. At large crime scenes where a murder may have taken place, dogs can soon find a hidden human body. They can even find hidden human remains at old crime scenes.

Crime scene investigators make good use of trained dogs.

Four-legged friend

Some **evidence** at a crime scene is **invisible,** such as the **scent** left behind by people. We all leave a trail of skin **cells,** hair, sweat, and other body oils, which dogs can detect. Dogs can even tell the difference between new and older scents.

A sniffer dog is soon on the scent of a crime.

invisible   cannot be seen

Searching the scene

Some murderers go to a lot of trouble to hide the body. In 2001, 36-year-old Kimberly Szumski went missing in Philadelphia. Her husband had killed and buried her. To make sure no one would find her, he put large concrete blocks on top of her grave. Then he built a brick wall on top with steel bars in it.

Months later, the police used dogs to search for Kimberly. Even though she was wrapped in plastic and buried deep underground, the dogs could smell her body and began barking. The police dug down and found the body. Kimberly's husband was arrested.

The nose of a detective

Some crime scene investigators use a machine that sucks up smells onto a scent pad. This can be freeze-dried and used years later if needed. It can collect scents left at the scene of a break-in and later be given to a dog to sniff. All the dog has to do is sniff out the right **suspect**!

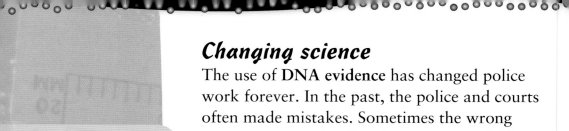

Changing science

The use of **DNA evidence** has changed police work forever. In the past, the police and courts often made mistakes. Sometimes the wrong person was **convicted** and even **executed.** Now science can make crime detection much more **accurate.** Like fingerprints, parts of each person's DNA are **unique.**

Matching a person's DNA to a crime has helped to solve many old murder cases. It can also help to show if human remains are related to another person. Sir Alec Jeffreys developed DNA tests in 1984. He first solved a murder with DNA in the United Kingdom in 1986 by proving a **suspect** was **innocent. Forensic** science was never the same again.

What is DNA?

DNA is a chemical that holds all the instructions that make you unique. It is found in every one of your cells. DNA is like a code locked in your **genes.** It makes you who you are.

DNA samples can be taken from saliva inside the mouth.

DNA   code in each person's genes that makes him or her different from anyone else

Tomorrow's world?

It can now be proven that blood, hair, body fluids, **cells,** or **tissue** found at a crime scene belong to a particular person. Suspects today have their fingerprints and a sample of DNA taken when they are arrested. Records are then stored on computer so they can be matched against other crimes.

Collecting DNA is just a matter of taking a sample of **saliva** from inside the mouth. One day, all babies may have this done at birth so that everyone in the world is recorded. Then any drop of blood, hair, or cells could be traced at the touch of a button. Do you think this is the best answer for solving crimes in the future?

Fast work

Databases now store DNA profiles of millions of people around the world. DNA from each new crime scene is stored. It is then matched with DNA profiles from other crimes. If a person has a criminal record, a computer can find or match his or her DNA information in a matter of seconds. Science is now making it much harder to get away with crime.

A scientist examines a DNA sample.

If you want to find out more about the criminal underworld, take a look at these books:

Dowswell, Paul. *Forensic Files: Investigating Murders*. Chicago: Heinemann, 2004.

Owen, David. *Police Lab: How Forensic Science Tracks Down and Convicts Criminals*. Westport, Conn.: Firefly, 2002.

Schulz, Karen. *Crime Scene Detective*. San Luis Obispo, CA: Dandy Lion, 2003.

Did you know?

In Australia it is a crime in some states to:
- own a mattress without a mattress licence;
- wear pink short-shorts after midday on Sundays;
- change a lightbulb unless you are an electrician!

Pigeons

Police in Belgium finally caught up with a man fourteen years after he murdered his wife. The man changed his name and moved in 1989. He was caught recently when a police officer spotted his photo in a pigeon breeders' magazine!

Criminal records

- The world's first speeding ticket was issued in Great Britain in 1896 to a man named Walter Arnold. He was traveling at 8 mph (13 km/h) in a 2 mph (3.25 km/h) zone.

- The most successful sniffer dog was a Labrador from the United States named Snag. He found 118 different hoards of hidden drugs worth an amazing $1 billion!

- The oldest person to be hanged was 82-year-old Allan Mair in 1843 Britain. He was hanged sitting down, since he was unable to stand.

- The world's largest safety-deposit-box robbery took place in 1976. A group of highly trained criminals stole more than $39 million worth of goods from a bank in the Middle East.

Tattoo

An armed robber from California was caught because of his "not-guilty" tattoo! Witnesses clearly remembered seeing the tattoo at the robbery. The man was picked up soon after his raid—while showing off his tattoo to locals.

accurate   exactly right, with no mistakes

analysis   careful study and examination

artery   tube in the body that carries blood from the heart

autopsy   examination of a dead body to find the cause of death

bacteria   tiny living things that can only be seen under a microscope

ballistics   science of guns and bullets

cartridge   shell around the gunpowder that fires a bullet

cast   to shape like something else using a mold

cell   tiny unit that is the building block of the body and its functions

convicted   proven guilty in court and sentenced

conviction   when a court finds someone guilty of a crime

convince   to persuade

crime lab   science laboratory in which evidence from crime scenes is studied

database   large amount of information stored on a computer

defense team   lawyers in court who try to show that a suspect is not guilty

dental   to do with teeth

digital photos   photos made using computer software rather than photographic film

dispose   to get rid of

dissolve   to break down into a liquid

DNA   code in each person's genes that makes him or her different from anybody else

evidence   facts pointing to what happened

executed   killed as a punishment

features   main parts of the face, such as the nose, eyes, and chin

fibers   tiny threads

forensic   detailed scientific investigation to help solve crimes

fracture   break or crack

gene   set of instructions inside all our cells

graphics   pictures made using computer technology

habitat   natural home of an animal

hit-and-run   when a driver runs down a person but does not stop

humerus   bone in the upper arm

identity   person's name and details

impression   mark or print left behind

innocent   not guilty

interfere   disturb or get in the way

intestine   part of the digestive system

intruder   burglar who breaks into someone's property

investigate   look for information about a crime

invisible   cannot be seen

jury group of people chosen to make a decision about whether or not someone is guilty

laboratory special room set up for scientific research

latex type of thin rubber

legal to do with the law

microscope instrument for magnifying tiny objects

mislead send someone in the wrong direction

mortuary place where dead bodies are kept until burial

pathologist person who studies disease and injury and their effects on the body

pathology study of disease and injury and their effects on the body

pelvis part of the skeleton, including the hips and lower back

pollen fine grains, like dust, made by a flower or tree

professor someone who has studied a subject to a very high level and teaches it to others, often at a university

prosecution team of lawyers who try to prove someone is guilty of a crime

ransom payment demanded for the release of a prisoner

reliable something that can be trusted

residue what is left over

rigid unable to bend

rigor mortis stiffening of the muscles that happens soon after death

saliva fluid made in the mouth

scent smell

sterile completely clean

suffocate to choke or kill by stopping breathing

sulfur yellow substance sometimes used to make gunpowder

suspect person who is thought to be responsible for a crime

suspicious seeming as if something wrong or criminal has happened

tissue soft parts of the body

toxic poisonous

trace very small mark, sign, or substance that is left behind

transfer pass from one place to another

unique only one of it in the whole world

vein tube in the body that carries blood to the heart

victim person who gets hurt or killed by a crime

vital very important

Index